Michelle D. Russell

An Experience Every Christian Must Have: From Darkness to Light

PublishAmerica
Baltimore

First printing

PublishAmerica has allowed this work to remain exactly as the author intended, verbatim, without editorial input.

The Scripture versions cited in this book are identified in Appendix 2.

ISBN: 1-60813-469-5
PUBLISHED BY PUBLISHAMERICA, LLLP
www.publishamerica.com
Baltimore

Printed in the United States of America

Dedication

I would like to dedicate *An Experience Every Christian Must Have: From Darkness to Light* to my father, Dave Russell, to my brothers: James Warner, David, Donald, Michael & Timothy Russell, to my friend, Daniel G. Dancy, to Sister Sharon Johnson; a dear friend, a true woman of God, who encourages me to live my life for the Lord, to Elder G. Craige Lewis; a man of God that has a powerful ministry; The Truth Behind Hip Hop, to all the homeless men and women assisted by From Darkness to Light (a nonprofit organization established to assist the homeless; http://www.fromdarkness2light.org), and to all the marvelous members of From Darkness to Light.

We are all at different levels in our walk with Christ. It is my desire that we all receive a "from darkness to light," experience and develop a personal relationship with the Lord. Coming from darkness to light is an awesome experience, but this experience is *impossible* to achieve without seeking God, having a relationship with Jesus Christ, and allowing the Holy Spirit to reside within you. This book is all about the experience of from darkness to light, what it means, and what must be done in order to achieve it.

1 John 3: 16-18

3:16 Hereby perceive we the love of God, because he laid down his life for us: and we ought to lay down our lives for the brethren.

3:17 But whoso hath this world's good, and seeth his brother have need, and shutteth up his bowels of compassion from him, how dwelleth the love of God in him?

3:18 My little children, let us not love in word, neither in tongue; but in deed and in truth.

Contents

An Experience Every Christian Must Have: From Darkness to Light

From Darkness to Light

I have decided to write this book because I have a story to tell. My name is Michelle Russell and I consider myself to be a freelance writer and speaker. I have not always had a desire to write or speak, but my life instantly changed in September of 2005, it was in September of 2005 that I began a "from darkness to light experience."

You ask me, what is a "from darkness to light" experience? This is when the Lord starts to draw you to him and you are able to see things clearly. Your eyes are opened. You are able to understand and discern spiritual matters. You acquire wisdom and knowledge that you did not have prior to your from darkness to light experience. You look at everything differently; what mattered and concerned you in the past do not matter anymore. Your priorities change and you look at people differently. You acquire the fruit of the spirit and become more patient and long-suffering. Your desire to witness, worship and praise the Lord becomes an invariable urge that you feel you have no restrain over. The Lord is constantly on your mind. You are constantly talking about Jesus and you sincerely desire to please Jehovah (God) in everything that you do. You determine that you have a mission or purpose in life and you set out to accomplish your mission or purpose with a serious passion. You make sacrifices and you give up things or do without things, if you feel it's according to God's will or purpose for your life.

My Story

I did not find the Lord, until I truly decided to seek him. I have been in the church my entire life and I never truly knew the Lord or his presence until September 2005. The person that I have become cannot believe that I walked around "blind" for 35 years without having a major wreck. I praise God for his mercy and his grace. In my youth, while attending a Baptist Church I was in the choir, and was a member of the Usher Board. My family converted from Baptist to Seventh Day Adventist when I was 16 years old; imagine being told at 16 that the Sabbath is Saturday and you have to go to church on Saturday instead of Sunday. No more doing what I wanted to do; hanging out with friends and going shopping on Saturday. I was very confused back then, but it has all become very clear to me as I sit here and type today.

I am currently attending a Seventh Day Adventist (SDA) Church and I am very active in the church. I have been a member of the SDA Church for 23 years. Prior to my "from darkness to light" experience I was a member of the Church Board, the Usher Board, and held the position of Adventist Youth (AY) Leader. Again, I have always been very involved in church, but "being in the church and being active in the church does not guarantee salvation." Although I was in the church for many years I was only going through the motions of playing church; it was a tradition for me. Going to church was just a formal process; I felt I was required to go. I wanted to please my parents. I had no real connection with or to Jehovah God; there was no personal relationship established. I did not enjoy service; church was very boring to me and I was always pleased when the services ended. It was difficult for me to pay attention to what was being discussed; my mind often drifted to other concerns; what I would do when church was over; wondering what my "boyfriend" or friends were doing while I was stuck in church. Yes, I said "boyfriend." I had a boyfriend and things were serious between us; we were doing things that were outside of God's will and I didn't have a problem with the life style I was living. I thought everything was fine. I thought I was intelligent; knew it all and had everything under control at the age of 16.

I had often heard people making comments about being born again, but I had no clue as to what they were talking about, nor did I realize what that statement really meant. I was in the church, but I had not had a born again experience, which I am now calling a "from darkness to light experience." I was going to church doing what I thought was acceptable in God's sight, but boy was I wrong. I did not realize how far a part from Jehovah God I was. I did not have a personal relationship with the Lord and I did not think anything was wrong with that. I did not communicate with the Lord on a regular basis and he was not the center of my life. My relationship with Jesus was not a priority to me. For more than 35 years I walked around with a blindfold on, and it has been due to God's Grace and Mercy that I am here to share this story.

We must stop playing church and be about our Heavenly Father's business. After you have read this book you will know what it is to have a "from darkness to light experience" or "to be born again." You will know what it is to be a true Christian, not just someone professing to be a Christian and living the life of a heathen. I feel it is essential that I address these issues because many do not realize that they are outside of the will of God, they cannot see. "I could not see." My assignment is to shed some light on this issue, so that many may see a flicker of light and *truly* seek the Lord, Jesus Christ.

In September of 2005, I watched a video entitled "The Truth Behind Hip Hop." The information on the video was presented by Elder G. Craig Lewis, a young man that has been given an assignment by God to preach the gospel and share a message regarding the truth behind hip hop. The message Elder Lewis shared was awesome and I instantly knew after listening to his message that a light bulb was on within me; there was a flicker of light that continued to intensify as I started to seek God.

I have to thank the Lord for using Elder G. Craig Lewis. The Lord used his ministry (his video) to change my life. His message caused me to question my religious conviction and my walk with Jesus Christ. I had questions that I wanted answered, so I went to the word (The Holy Bible). When I turned to the word and really started to seek God, I found him and I was born again. "I went from darkness to light." The bible says, "ask, and it shall be given you; **seek, and ye shall find;** knock, and it shall be opened unto you." (Mat 7:7 and

Luke 11:9) "Therefore if any man be in Christ, he is a new creature: old things are passed away; behold, all things are become new" (II Corinthians 5:17). The Lord allowed the Holy Spirit to fall upon me and instantly I went from darkness to light; I have not been the same since. I would compare my feeling or experience to that of the Apostle Peter; when he was transformed after Pentecost (Acts 2:14-41) and filled with the Holy Spirit; he preached powerfully to a crowd and as a result of the Holy Spirit working through his preaching he was able to baptize 3,000 people or the experience of the Apostle Paul when he tells of his conversion to King Agrippa; Paul was transformed after he had an encounter with Jesus (Acts: 26: 12-23). Jesus said to Paul, "But rise, and stand upon thy feet: for I have appeared unto thee for this purpose, to make thee a minister and a witness both of these things which thou hast seen, and of those things in the which I will appear unto thee; 17) Delivering thee from the people, and from the Gentiles, unto whom now I send thee, 18) To open their eyes, and to turn them **from darkness to light**, and from the power of Satan unto God, that they may receive forgiveness of sins, and inheritance among them which are sanctified by faith that is in me (Acts 26: 16-18)."

I believe that because I was willing and seeking the Lord, he revealed himself to me. He became real when I became serious and said, "Yes Lord." God did not come into my life until I seriously desired him to do so. The Lord knew that I was sincere when I asked him to come into my life and make his presence known. He revealed himself to me, and my life changed. It's very essential that we seek God for direction. The bible says, "But from there you will seek the LORD your God, and *you will find Him if you search for Him with all your heart and all your soul* (Deuteronomy 4:29 NAS)." The scriptures also advise us to, "Trust in the LORD with all thine heart; and lean not unto thine own understanding. In all thy ways acknowledge him, and he shall direct thy paths (Proverbs 3: 5-6)."

Prior to my "from darkness to light experience," I was in the church, but I was lost! How can this be? Saints we have gotten so far away from what God intended for us. This world has a way of making good look bad and bad look good. We are to accepting of the ways of the world. We are allowing and tolerating too much nonsense in our lives; our conversations, our music, our entertainment it's "all" inappropriate and outside the will of God. I was not able to see and focus clearly until I removed the junk from my life and turned to the Bible for guidance. For example I was going to church on a regular basis, very active in the church, but also very active in the world. I was what one would call straddling the fence, one foot in the church, and one foot out.

From an early age it was not uncommon for me to tell lies and take things that did not belong to me. I did not have a problem with stealing and/or lying about it. I remember being a young child, in the first grade and I was often getting into trouble for fighting and taking things from other kids. I was horrible during my elementary years. I was a little rascal. Although I was really bad during elementary school, by the time I got to middle school I was a model student; often on the merit and honor roll. I didn't bother anyone and I was considered a peacemaker. I even received the citizenship medallion (an award presented by the school faculty) when I was in the seventh/eighth grade. My teachers saw something good in me. I took a big interest in school and education while in middle school. I managed to stay out of trouble in both middle and high school, but by the time I got to high school (9th grade) I was interested in boys and my grades suffered; I started to get Cs on my report card, which was something I never allowed in middle school. Shortly after graduating from high school in 1988 I found myself in trouble with the law. I will discuss more about my encounter with the law in Chapter 10 (Be Content).

My Christian character was far from perfect. Christians are not perfect people, but we should be striving to obtain a Christ like character. I was professing to be a Christian, but was not making any real effort to be a Christian. I would have conversations with individuals, engaging in the latest gossip, instead of discouraging it. A Christian should not gossip or be a part of a negative conversation. A Christian should edify and encourage others. I was listening to the wrong type of music; if it doesn't glorify God it's not worth listening to. Church we have to be very careful what we listen to. "In order to keep your thoughts pure you must keep your mind on spiritual things." A lot of the music promoted today will not allow us to keep our minds pure, due to the foul lyrics, sexual content, suggestive and subliminal messages that are contained in the songs. My choice of entertainment was also an issue; I was watching movies Rated R, X, Horror, Super Natural, etc. I would host parties with alcoholic beverages and was considered a social drinker, having one or two daiquiris or mixed drinks every now and then. This type of behavior is not acceptable behavior for a professed Christian.

I have determined that if professed Christians continue to

live like the world they will never determine their purpose; they will never be content or fulfilled; they will constantly be chasing the wind. A "from darkness to light" experience involves a transformation, an encounter with the Holy Spirit. We must allow the Holy Spirit to reside within us. A person cannot be born again, unless they die to the things of this world. My life has completely changed since I allowed the Lord to have his way. I am finding that it is much easier to serve the Lord now that I have surrendered to his will. I am much happier; things are no longer a struggle for me. Why do we try to fight against God? Do we not realize that we are fighting a losing battle? We can't beat God! We must become radical in our obedience to God, and then we will win.

Some people may think that my ideas are extreme, and that could be because they have not been born again. When you have been born again your desire is to please God, he becomes your #1 priority in life. If God is not the priority in your life, you need to examine yourself and determine where you stand. Are you a Christian? Some may feel that they have control over what they watch and listen to, but if you are allowing yourself to listen to music and watch movies or TV shows that do not glorify the Lord you are not in control, but are being controlled. God wants to fill us; he wants to bring us to a higher level, but we have so much stuff blurring our vision; so much stuff in the way. We are not spending enough "quality" time with God. I challenge you to get rid of the distractions (past-times; chatting, music, movies, etc) the things that are keeping you from God. Seek him, study his word, pray, and witness a "from darkness to light" experience in your life. It may feel like a big sacrifice at first, but in time you will recognize your gain and come to appreciate it all; it is truly a blessing in disguise. The Lord wants to fill you; he wants to give you the fruit of the spirit. God knows what is best for us, if we would only trust him and allow his will to be done in our lives we would come to understand that he is God and he knows best; the Psalmist says, "Know you that the LORD he is God: it is he that has made us, and not we ourselves; we are his people, and the sheep of his pasture" (Psalm 100:3). God made us and he knows what is best for us. "He that hath an ear, let him hear what the Spirit saith unto the churches; To him that overcometh will I give to eat of the tree of life, which is in the midst of the paradise of God." (Revelation 2:7)

Jesus said, "and I, if I be lifted up from the earth, will draw all men unto me." (John 12:32). Now is the time that we allow the Lord to be lifted up. We have got to get out of the way. So many of us are trying to get the glory and we are in the way, and therefore people cannot see Jesus. Let's commit to doing the Lords will. Let's focus on reaching the people, in order to hasten his coming. It is my prayer that we obtain wisdom and knowledge, and that the Lord will direct our paths.

Wake Up!

"*For my thoughts are not your thoughts, neither are your ways my ways,*" declares the LORD. "As the heavens are higher than the earth, **so are my ways higher than your ways and my thoughts than your thoughts.**" (Isaiah 55:8-9)

Brethren, wake up and understand that everything happens for a reason and no matter what you are going through, be assured that God is in it. For the bible says, "And we know that in all things God works for the good of those who love him, who have been called according to his purpose (Romans 8:28)." We may not understand why things happen the way they do, and it is not for us to understand everything. Just know that what ever you are going through, it will pass and Jehovah God will work it out for you, just hang in there and trust in the Lord. All things can be achieved through Jesus Christ, he has our best interest at heart, for he hath said, "I will never leave thee, nor forsake thee (Hebrews 13:5)." He assures us that "There hath no temptation taken you but such as is common to man: but God is faithful, who will not suffer you to be tempted above that ye are able; but will with the temptation also make a way to escape, that ye may be able to bear it (I Cor. 10:13)."

Jesus said unto Thomas, I am the way, the truth, and the life: no man cometh unto the Father, but by me. (John 14:6) Brethren, it's time to wake up! Our prayer should be that the Lord would give us discernment, wisdom and knowledge. If we do not seek God with our whole heart, we will never find him. God will not draw us to him, if we are not seeking him. The Bible is very clear about what we must do, in order to find God. There is nothing we cannot do, if we allow the Lord Jesus to dwell within us. With Christ in us we will be content with what we have, therefore we will cease chasing after things in this life that do not matter. We will have the power to stop indulging in any habit-forming practice. We would be able to over come any struggle because Jesus will be in control, not us; therefore the sky is the limit to what you can do through Christ. "He that hath an ear, let him hear (Revelation 2:7)."

So many are broken; there is so much pain. People are heartbroken, depressed, they have mental illness, they struggle with substance abuse, death, sorry, grief, loneliness, stress, sickness, disease, poverty, hunger, and so many other ailments. Do we not realize that Christ can heal us from all these issues? Do we not want to be healed or do we simply not know how to obtain healing? It's not a mystery. The answer is simple, **first:** trust and believe in God. Make the Lord your savior and ask him to come into your heart. You must be sincere when you ask the Lord to come into your heart. The Bible says, "According to your faith be it unto you (Matthew 9:29). All things whatsoever ye shall ask in prayer, believing, ye shall receive (Matthew 21:22)." **Second:** You must put God first in your life; God must be your first priority; nothing, nobody or anything can come before God. If you are not currently at this level, pray that God will help you to put him first in everything that you think, say or do. The Bible clearly tells us that the Lord is a jealous God (Exodus 20:5), therefore do not put anything before him; he is possessive of the worship and service that belongs to him. Make sure to honor him. Do not put your spouse, your children, your job/career, your house, your car, your money, or anything else before him. **Third:** Ask for his forgiveness, and then ask for his blessing. God will answer your prayer. The Bible says, "What things so ever ye desire, when ye pray, believe that ye receive them and ye shall have them (Mark 11:24)." Understand that the Lord will answer the prayers of his children. You must pray and study his word; this will bring you closer to him and it will give you peace, the fruit of the spirit. Ask yourself; are you a child of God? If you are not sincere and you are not striving to be Christ like then you can't count on him to answer your prayers. His words are clear, "If ye abide in me, and my word abide in you, ye shall ask what ye will and it shall be done unto you (John 15:7). Pray, believe, rejoice, and sing praises to God because he has answered your prayers. Take him at his word. He is faithful that promised (Heb. 10:23)."

People, it is time that we wake up and start minding the things that are important. It is essential that we have a relationship with Jesus Christ. Understand that nothing in this world matters, except for what we do for Jesus Christ. Your goal in this life should be to determine what God would have you to do. I often pray that the Lord will direct my path and that he would reveal his plans to me. The Lord has given me wisdom and knowledge because I have prayed for it. I have asked the Lord to direct my path because I want to be sure that I am doing his will.

Some times we have to suffer the consequences of bad decisions and some times bad things happen to good people, if you have a relationship with the Lord you will get through anything that comes your way, but understand that there is no reason for us to be in a constant state of depression. If you are constantly depressed, you must examine your attitude because you are your worst enemy. Believe it or not you; your attitude has a lot to do with your feelings of depression; it is all in your attitude; it really is. In other words, you must learn how to make lemons into lemonade. Think positive; focus on the positive in any bad situation. Thank God for his blessings, especially the ones that you take for granted every day. Do not dwell on the bad. God can give you the power to do this. If it is your desire to overcome, you can. God can make this easy for you, but you have to try and you have to practice this on a regular basis; any time you think of something negative or you start to complain about something, immediately ask for God's forgiveness and ask that he would give you the strength not to be negative or not to complain, or ask him to take you out of a depressed state, and then start praising his Holy name. Thank him for any and everything that you can think of. This takes practice, but it can become second nature.

We must wake up and realize that we were made to worship and praise the Lord. We were not made to sit around being heartbroken, depressed, struggling with mental illness, with substance abuse, stress, sickness, disease, and so many other ailments. Believe me when I say that if we would truly honor, worship, and praise the Lord as we were created to do, then we would see a major decrease in these types of problems mentioned. We would be asking the question: Stress and depression, what is that? Believe me when I say, "We have all these ailments because we do not know how to worship and praise the Lord." We are to busy complaining; too much complaining and not enough praising. We are seeking and searching for a cure to our ailments; taking all kinds of medications, going to and fro seeking treatment with no success. We do not even consider that the Master Physician has the cure. He has told us what we need to do in order to be healed, but either we are not listening or we just do not understand his instruction. Wake up before it is too late. God wants to give us the fruit of the spirit; he wants to bless us, but he will not force it upon us, we have to ask for it. He is waiting for us to ask. So many of us are wearing blind folds and don't even realize we need the Holy Spirit. It is my prayer that you will receive a from darkness to light experience. Open your eyes. Wake up!

Know the Lord for Yourself

"Study to shew thyself approved unto God, a workman that needeth not to be ashamed, rightly dividing the word of truth." (II Timothy 2:15)

In today's world there are so many religions, so many denominations. There are all sorts of teachings being taught. Christians, we must study for ourselves. We must understand the Bible for ourselves because we will be accountable for our own salvation and during the time of judgment we will not be able to say that we did not know or understand that certain things we were taught were wrong or outside of God's will. We will not be able to blame it on someone else or use the Pastor as an escape goat for not knowing. According to II Timothy 2:15, we are responsible for studying the Bible and understanding it, so I encourage you to study your Bibles and learn what thus saith the Lord for yourself.

Brethren if you are in a church that does not encourage you to read and study your Bibles, than you should question this practice. Could it be that someone may want you to be ignorant to the word of God? It is not wise for you to rely on the church or the pastor to interpret the word of God for you. It is your responsibility to read and study the word of God for yourself. There is nothing wrong with going to church and hearing a sermon or allowing the minister to speak to you, but it is your responsibility to make sure that what you are hearing and what you believe is fact. If you believe something you need to make sure that the teachings are coming straight from the Bible.

If you are in a church where the Pastor is constantly preaching prosperity messages and he is not feeding your soul when it comes to all other aspects of the Bible, then you need to determine if you are in the right church. Understand that religion can be, and it is considered big business. There is a lot of money involved. The Bible says that the love of money is the root of all-evil (I Timothy 6:10). Many individuals are motivated by money and some within the church will prey upon you. Understand that you could be their means for obtaining the money they so desperately desire. I encourage you to read a copy of Wolves in the American Church, written by Sharon Johnson (See Appendix 1). This book will shed some light on the issue of pulpit predators. I encourage you to read and study your Bible. Pray that God will give you wisdom and knowledge, so that you can understand his word. Pray for discernment, so that others are not able to take advantage of you, and so that you are able to make the right decisions when it comes to your spiritual walk with the Lord.

We spend so much time chasing after material things; money, cars, houses, and land that we forget about Jesus. We are so overwhelmed and consumed by our jobs/careers, education, families, and friends that we have no time for Jesus. We are so busy that we do not take the time to study our Bibles and pray. Not realizing that all the things we are focusing on has no power to save us. The most important thing (Jehovah God) is often our last priority. We read and study all types of secular novels and books, while the book of life; the Bible sits on a shelf collecting dust or lay hidden some where in a drawer or in storage. We can't know who God is, if we do not take the time to learn about him; it is up to us to get to know him. We fail to realize that the only thing that truly matters is what we do for Christ; everything else is in vain. God's word is full of insight and wisdom. In order to have the Wisdom of Solomon we must study the Bible. Wisdom is the principal thing; therefore get wisdom and in all your getting, get understanding (Proverbs 4:7).

Do you have a personal relationship with the Lord? Do you know the Lord? Do you feel that it is important for you to have a relationship with God? These are simple questions, but very important questions that everyone should ponder. If you answered no to the first two questions that is okay because we are all at different levels in our walk with Christ and God understands that. He works with all of us differently, therefore the time it takes for you to come to the Lord maybe different from the amount of time that it takes for someone else to come to the Lord. That is why we all should be thankful for God's Mercy and his Grace. God is long suffering and his time is not our time (Isaiah 55:89). He gives us so many chances to come; he gives us chance, after chance, after chance. God knows the heart of each individual and he knows whether or not an individual will eventually surrender his heart, and he knows exactly when that individual will do so. The essential question is, "Do you feel that it is important for you to have a relationship with God?" If you answered no, then you have a problem because you do not recognize that you need the Lord and you cannot be saved without the Lord. If you answered yes, then there is hope because God can work with you, if you are willing to allow him to do so.

If it is your desire to have a relationship with the Lord, simply pray and ask him to come into your heart. Say this simple prayer, "Lord, please come into my heart and reveal yourself to me. Lord, help me to have a closer walk with you, help me to live my life according to your will, and give me the strength and the power to be what you would have me to be. In the name of Jesus I pray, Amen." If you say this simple prayer and you are sincere, God will reveal himself to you. He will start to draw you towards him; suddenly you may have a desire to read the bible or go to church; that is the Holy Spirit working on you. You will need to work on developing your personal relationship with the Lord. When you hear him calling, harden not your heart; if you have a thought to do something spiritual, which may not be a normal thought for you, surrender to your thoughts because it is the Holy Spirit giving you those type of thoughts; he is trying to call you into the presence of God. Open your heart and receive him. Talk with God as you would talk to a friend. Talk to him as often as possible. The bible says we should pray without ceasing (I Thessalonians 5:17), therefore you cannot talk too much or too long. God will keep you in perfect peace if you keep your mind on him (Isaiah 26:3).

You must have a personal relationship with the Lord; it is not enough to simply attend church and profess to be a Christian, you have to know the Lord. You have to know what God is requiring of you. It must pain you when you sin against God. If you establish a relationship with the Lord and you get to know him it will pain you to sin. You will feel bad when you do anything that is outside of the will of God, therefore once you get to this point it will be a struggle for you to do anything wrong because you will be convicted by the Holy Spirit any time you attempt to do something that is not the will of God. The conviction of doing God's will, will become so severe; it will permeate your mind and will overcome your thoughts of wrongdoing. When you allow God to have his will in your life this becomes a natural and easy process; there is no longer a struggle for you. Remember we were created in the image of God (Genesis 1:27). We are a representation, a likeness of God; therefore the more we behave or function like God the better we will feel.

We need God whether we know it or not; we need to have a relationship with him more than we need water to drink or air to breath. It is essential that you know the Lord for yourself. Again, it's not enough to say that I am a member of this or that church or to say that I am a good person; I go to work, pay my taxes and I do not bother anyone. You better know the Lord. You must know the Lord in order to do his will. You need to know his likes and his dislikes. You must communicate with him; you must praise and worship him. You cannot sit idle, nor can you keep tradition (playing church) and expect the Lord to recognize you. If you do not establish a personal relationship with him and do his will, he will not acknowledge you. He will tell you to depart from him because he never knew you (Matthew 7:21-23). Your relationship with him should be closer than any other; now think about what was just said. Your relationship with him should be closer than any other. Think about the people in your life that you are really close to; your husband, wife, mother, father, sister, brother, friend. Your relationship with the Lord should be closer than any of these relationships, if you find that your relationship with the Lord is lacking substance than you need to start talking to him; start praying and studying; start communicating with him on a regular basis, until you are talking to him all day, on a daily basis. If you are not holding a verbal conversation with someone, then you should be praising the Lord or talking to him in thought; this type of behavior is what will build your relationship with the Lord. The more you talk to God the better you will know him. You will establish a relationship with him by talking to him. It may not be easy at first and it may feel awkward when you start talking to God. You may not know what to say, and that is fine. You do not have to use any fancy words or anything; just talk to him as you would talk to a friend. He is there and he is listening to you. Pour your heart out to God on a regular basis. Some people only pray to God at night when they get ready to go to bed. Listen, and listen good you should be communicating with God all throughout the day. It's good to have a set time for meditation and prayer and that should be something you do every day, but don't wait until bedtime to talk to God. If you communicate with him on a regular basis, you will start to trust in God, you will feel his presence and you will start to feel him moving in your life. I can't stress how important it is for you to communicate with God, and to establish a personal relationship with him. Do these simple things that I have suggested and feel the Lord become real in your life. Feel the presence of the Lord.

Let Your Light Shine

"You are the light of the world. A city that is set on a hill cannot be hidden. Nor do they light a lamp and put it under a basket, but on a lamp stand, and it gives light to all who are in the house. Let your light so shine before men, that they may see your good works and glorify your Father in heaven." (Matthew 5:14-16 NKJV)

After we are converted we are to let our light shine. Jesus said to Peter, "Simon, Simon, behold, Satan hath desired to have you, that he may sift you as wheat: 32) But I have prayed for thee, that thy faith fail not: and when thou art converted, strengthen thy brethren (Luke 22:31-32)." Christians must let their light shine before men, so that others may see their good works and glorify the heavenly father. It's not about us; it's all about Jesus, our Lord and savior. We were created to glorify the Lord. Most of us have become self-centered and we have made our own agendas the focus. We must put God first and be about his business. God knows what is best for us, if we would just live our lives according to his will we would be better off.

By letting our light shine we can have positive effects on

God's people. People are watching you, especially if you profess to be a Christian. People are watching to see how you live your life as a professed Christian, watching to see if God's power is working in your life. People want to know how Christians are different from anybody else; therefore Christians must let their light shine, so that others can see how they are different. True Christians will have the fruit of the spirit; they will have love, joy, peace, longsuffering, gentleness, goodness, faith, meekness, and temperance. If Christians are not able to display the spirit that only God can give them, it is obvious that they are not in Christ. The Bible says, "Thou wilt keep him in perfect peace, whose mind is stayed on thee: because he trusteth in thee (Isaiah 26:3). The Bible also says, you shall know them by their fruits (Matthew 7:16); wherefore by their fruits you shall know them (Matthew 7:20).

It is not always easy being a Christian, actually it is often a struggle to live in this world and be a true Christian. Christians are constantly struggling with themselves to pick good over evil. Understand that a persons flesh (the carnal mind) wants to sin. We want to do what makes our flesh feel good, but Christians choose to live a disciplined life, such as they choose to live a life pleasing to God; they want to be within the will of God. God wants us to be perfect. Jesus was perfect. Living a Christ like life is living a perfect life, just like Jesus did. It is no easy task to live a perfect life. The Bible informs that all have sinned, and come short of the glory of God (Romans 3:23), therefore it is impossible for any man to be perfect, but through Jesus Christ we can strive to be perfect. Our goal should be to always strive to live like Christ, but if we happen to sin (fall or make a mistake) in any area, we should ask for forgiveness, then forgive ourselves for falling and try, and try again, if necessary to be the person that God has called us to be. When a Christian is striving to live like Christ and they are in constant prayer it is much easier for them to achieve the task of living like Christ; God gives them the strength and the power to do so.

God has provided us a savior, through Jesus Christ. Jesus came and died on the cross for our sins, so that we could be saved. Without God's sacrifice we could not be saved. His death on the cross allows our sins, transgressions and inequities to be forgiven. God knows our heart and he knows if we are truly repentant/sorry for the sins that we have committed, therefore if we confess our sins he is faithful and just to forgive us of our sins, and to cleanse us from all unrighteousness (I John 1:9). It is important for Christians to gain the victory over the sin in their life. Christians are to be an example to others. We are to encourage one another to live holy lives and we are to be obedient to God. We do not want to be a hindrance to our fellow brother and sisters. We have to live by example; practice what we preach. People will respect you, if you prove to have integrity. Some people may not like you, but they will have respect for you and the honorable way you carry yourself could have a positive impact on the people that are watching.

Keep a positive attitude; try not to complain. Always let it be known that you trust in the Lord and that your peace comes from him. People need to know why you are full of joy. Let them know that God has bestowed upon you the fruit of the spirit. If God has blessed you, don't be afraid to sing praises to God; shout it to the mountaintops. Let everyone know where your blessings come from. Some times Christians seem to be afraid to let others know that God has blessed them and they some times act as if it is taboo to talk about the goodness of God, especially in the workplace. We need holy boldness in the 21st Century. We have to let our light shine. If we were to let our light shine it would hasten the Lords return. We have to stop acting as if we are ashamed (uncomfortable, embarrassed, or uncertain) of God. The Bible says that if you are ashamed of Jesus and his words than he will be ashamed of you when he comes in his father's glory with his Holy Angels (Luke 9:26). If you are afraid to give honor and glory to God, you are in jeopardy of losing your soul. The Bible is clear, if you disown Jesus before man, he will disown you before his father in heaven (Matthew 10:33). This is why it is so important to have a relationship with the Lord; you need to know what God requires of you. Satan does not want you to let your light shine. He wants you to be lost; he knows that if you refuse to acknowledge the Lord, if you refuse to tell others about Jesus, he knows that you will be lost. You may feel that you are a good person, but that is not good enough; you have to let your light shine. You have to tell people about Jesus. Tell people how good God has been to you. If you have a testimony don't be afraid to share it with others. Share with others the difference God has made in your life, so that they might seek God and be saved. Do not be ashamed of the Gospel (II Timothy 1:8-10). It's all about winning souls for Christ.

What type of example are you setting as a Christian? Are you helping people in need? Are you showing love? Do people on your job or in your community even know that you are a Christian? The apostle Paul said it best when he said, follow my example as I follow the example of Christ (I Corinthians 11:1). We all know what type of example Jesus Christ was. We are to love one another; God is calling us to put others before ourselves. Scripture actually says, "Hereby perceive we the love of God, because he laid down his life for us: and we ought to lay down our lives for the brethren (1 John 3: 16)." We should have so much love for one another that we would be willing to lay down our lives and die for one another. Can Christians of the 21st Century love like God has called us to love one another? We have become a selfish nation and not many are willing to love the way the Bible has instructed us to love. It is easy to love those that love us, but it is hard to love those who hate us (Luke 6:32). It is expected that we would love those who love us. Can we love those that hate us?

Dr. Martin Luther King Jr. was a man of God and he understood the Bible concept of Luke 6:32. Dr. King taught nonviolence. Dr. King realized that God would fight his battles, if he would be obedient to the Lord's word. God's word says, "for it is written, vengeance is mine; I will repay, saith the Lord" (Romans 12:19). The Bible also says, "Do not say I'll pay you back for this wrong! Wait for the Lord, and He will deliver you (Proverbs 20:22)." Again, Dr. Martin Luther King Jr. understood scripture and he was trying to teach this concept to those who were being oppressed. He was teaching the oppressed not to retaliate against their oppressors, but to protest nonviolently. Dr. King knew that God would take care of the problem. In his "I Have a Dream" speech he said, "Let us not seek to satisfy our thirst for freedom by drinking from the cup of bitterness and hatred." He said, "I have a dream that one day every valley shall be exalted, every hill and mountain shall be made low, the rough places will be made plain, and the crooked places will be made straight, and the glory of the Lord shall be revealed, and all flesh shall see it together." He said, "This is our hope. This is the faith that I go back to the South with. With this faith we will be able to hew out of the mountain of despair a stone of hope. With this faith we will be able to transform the jangling discords of our nation into a beautiful symphony of brotherhood. With this faith we will be able to work together, to pray together, to struggle together, to go to jail together, to stand up for freedom together, knowing that we will be free one day."

Dr. King had a dream and his dream has come true. People who witnessed and participated in the Civil Rights Movement of the 1950's and 1960's found it hard to believe that Dr. King's dream would ever come true, but his dream has come true. He dreamed of racial equality. He dreamed that "black men as well as white men, would be guaranteed the unalienable rights of life, liberty, and the pursuit of happiness." He dreamed that "little black boys and black girls will be able to join hands with little white boys and white girls as sisters and brothers." His dream has come to pass; race relations are much better today, and on January 20, 2009 Barack Hussein Obama was inaugurated as the first African American President of the United States of America. Dr. King had faith and he prayed for racial equality, and in the 21st Century his dream is being fulfilled. Racial Relations are being strengthened every day, week, month, and year that goes by.

Jesus Christ is the perfect example of I John 3:16. Through the strength of Jesus Christ leaders such as Dr. King has prevailed. Don't be ashamed of the Lord, he can and will work miracles through you. He will see you through any adversity. He is coming back again, and when he comes in the clouds of glory his reward will be with him. Choose to let your light shine, be a help to others.

What Must Be Done?

"The natural man receiveth not the things of the Spirit of God: for they are foolishness unto him: neither can he know them, because they are spiritually discerned (1 Corinthians 2:14)." "Marvel not that I said unto thee, Ye must be born again (John 3:7)." The Apostle Paul longed for the purity and righteousness that of himself he could not obtain; he cried out "O wretched man that I am! Who shall deliver me from this body of death (Romans 7:24)?"

The Lamb of God; Jesus Christ is the answer for deliverance. We must receive Jesus Christ if we are to be delivered. We can be restored and all sins can be forgiven through the blood of Jesus Christ; through Christ, earth is reconnected with Heaven. Sinners must recognize that they need the Lord. We must repent and then confess our sins. We must yield our hearts unto God and be consecrated unto him. If we are going to be saved we must repent. John the Baptist and the Apostles preached it. Peter said, we must repent, and be converted, that your sins may be blotted out (Acts 3:19). We must repent and turn away from sin. We will not see a real change in our lives until we repent and turn away from sin in our heart. We must be sincere and feel a sorrow in our hearts for committing sin and we must turn away from it and conviction will take hold of our heart and mind. If we repent and yield our will to the Holy Spirit, we will experience from darkness to light. The hidden things of darkness will be made manifest. The Lord will remove the blindfolds and you will be able to discern spiritual things; even the Bible will become clear to you; this is God's promise (see 1 Corinthians 2:14).

We have no power to control our thoughts, desires, and actions, but God gives us free will, we have the power of decision. If we would choose to serve God he will give us the power to control our thoughts, desires, and actions. He will take control of our hearts and he will work a good thing in us; to will and to do according to his good pleasure. If it were your will, God would bring your entire being under the control of the Holy Spirit. The Apostle Paul spoke to the saints of Ephesus and he said, "(3) Blessed *be* the God and Father of our Lord Jesus Christ, who has blessed us with every spiritual blessing in the heavenly *places* in Christ, (4) just as He chose us in Him before the foundation of the world, that we should be holy and without blame before Him in love, (5) having predestined us to adoption as sons by Jesus Christ to Himself, according to the good pleasure of His will (Ephesians 1:3-5)." The Bible also says, "(20) Now the God of peace, that brought again from the dead our Lord Jesus, that great shepherd of the sheep, through the blood of the everlasting covenant, (21) Make you perfect in every good work to do his will, working in you that which is well pleasing in his sight, through Jesus Christ; to whom be glory for ever and ever. Amen. (Hebrews

13:20-21)." It is God's desire that we choose goodness and holiness, and that we would be in harmony with him. God does not force his will on us; he allows us to choose. If we choose him he will perfect our characters and our desire will become his desire.

It's up to us to make a choice to accept God. After we have made the choice of acceptance we then have to believe. When Jesus was on this earth he healed those who believed. The Bible says, "But without faith it is impossible to please him: for he that cometh to God must believe that he is, and that he is a rewarder of them that diligently seek him (Hebrews 11:6)." If you desire to be born again, you must act on that desire; take steps towards the Lord, and the Lord will give you the desire to change. He will give you strength and power, and you will be transformed. If you confess your sins, turn your life over to the Lord, and believe he will make you whole, as soon as you do this God will began a new work in you and you will be made whole. You are redeemed and made whole, through this simple act of faith. "As you therefore have received Christ Jesus the Lord, so walk ye in him (Colossians 2:6)."

Our heavenly Father loves us with an everlasting and unconditional love. His word says, "I have loved thee with an everlasting love: therefore with loving-kindness have I drawn thee (Jeremiah 31:3)." God is awaiting our call; as soon as we call upon him he is there to draw us towards him. We cannot come to the Lord unless he draws us, but we cannot be drawn unless we call upon the Lord; the ball is in our court. Jesus died on the cross for our sins, therefore we have a savior and he is constantly interceding for us. Jesus sacrifice allows us to be restored. Take a step towards the Lord and he will draw you closer. Repent, ask for forgiveness, consecrate yourself to God and believe that God will forgive and restore you. Each day ask the Lord to draw you closer and believe that he will, and then witness a from darkness to light experience in your life.

Love

The bible mentions a story regarding a Pharisee, who asked Jesus, *"Master, which is the great commandment in the law? Jesus said unto him, Thou shalt love the Lord thy God with all thy heart, and with all thy soul, and with all thy mind. This is the first and great commandment."* (Matthew 22:36-38) While speaking with the disciples, Jesus also advised, *"A new commandment I give unto you, That ye love one another; as I have loved you, that ye also love one another."* (John 13:34)

Jesus gave a commandment for us to love one another. It is very important to the Lord that we love each other. God is love and that is why he was able to die on the cross for our sins, even though we were not worthy of his love. We are aware of the example that Jesus Christ left for us. We are to strive to have Christ like characters.

I knew that I was witnessing a From Darkness to Light experience in my life when I noticed the way I had started treating others. I was much more loving and compassionate towards others. I became very sensitive to peoples struggles; I had never really cared prior to being touched with the Holy Spirit. Again, God is love and the Holy Spirit is very sensitive. You will feel the Holy Spirit when you allow his Spirit to reside in you. I was able to actually feel his presence. I would start crying instantly if I heard about or witnessed people suffering or struggling in any way. This behavior was very foreign or unfamiliar to me because I had never been a sensitive person prior to receiving the Holy Spirit.

My mother passed away in January of 1997. I loved my mother dearly; she was my best friend and she meant the world to me, but I did not cry at her funeral. I was able to suppress my feelings and keep my composure in public. I felt that I had control of my feelings. After being filled with the Holy Spirit I became very sensitive. I have a strong sense of awareness and I have compassion for people. I can sense or tell when people are hurting or going through things and it causes me to cry; it's as if the Holy Spirit in me can feel their pain. I am very concerned about others. I cry when I am happy or sad and I never did that before. Sometimes I cry during Church services, just thinking about how good God has been to me. Sometimes I simply feel the overwhelming sense of the Holy Spirit's presence and it is such a joy. I feel high (lifted up) when the Holy Spirit is moving; it's an awesome feeling. I do not think any addiction can compare to being addicted to the Holy Spirit.

After being touched by the Holy Spirit I had a passion and strong desire to work with the homeless. I helped to start a non-profit organization, known as From Darkness to Light. Our Bible text for the organization is I John 3:16-18. The organization was founded on this belief. The members of the organization all feel that we should love and help one another. If we would keep the commandment that Jesus gave us in John 13:34 this world would be a better place.

1 John 3: 16-18

3:16 Hereby perceive we the love of God, because he laid down his life for us: and we ought to lay down our lives for the brethren.

3:17 But whoso hath this world's good, and seeth his brother have need, and shutteth up his bowels of compassion from him, how dwelleth the love of God in him?

3:18 My little children, let us not love in word, neither in tongue; but in deed and in truth.

Working with the homeless has been a joy for me. The Lord uses my experiences to keep me humble and thankful. Prior to working with the homeless I took a lot for granted. I am so thankful that the Lord allowed me to see the condition that I was in. He allowed me to see that I was selfish and ungrateful for all the blessings that he had given to me. When I was able to see myself clearly, I did not like what I was seeing. I was disgusted with myself; how could I have been so blind and so ungrateful for all of God's blessings. I felt so unworthy and so ashamed for the way I had lived my life. God had blessed me with a loving family, good health, a good job, a nice home, a nice automobile to drive, and I was often complaining about any and every insignificant thing. I was getting upset and wasting lots of time and energy over things that didn't even matter. I was pretty superficial prior to yielding my will to God. Now that I am a new creature in Christ, old things are past away, and all things have become new (II Corinthians 5:17). I am so thankful that God is love and that he is long suffering.

According to the scriptures, God is calling for us to love one another. He wants us to treat each other like he treats us. For many of us this is almost impossible for us to do. This world has conditioned us to be full of pride, arrogant, self-centered, and in some ways uncaring. Today we love our pets more than we do our neighbor. There is nothing wrong with loving our pets, but God calls us to treat our neighbors as ourselves. Many of us are lacking in this area, and we're often outside of God's will. God would have us to be humble people and love one another.

The Bible says, "If I have a faith that can move mountains, but have not love, I am nothing. If I give all I possess to the poor and surrender my body to the flames, but have not love, I gain nothing. Love is patient, and love is kind. It does not envy, it does not boast, it is not proud. It is not rude, it is not self-seeking, it is not easily angered, it keeps no record of wrongs. Love does not delight in evil but rejoices with the truth. It always protects, always trusts, always hopes, and always perseveres. Love never fails (I Corinthians 13:2-8)." "He that loveth not knoweth not God; for God is love (1 John 4:8)."

There are three Greek words that describe love. "Philia" which means friendship love, "eros" which means sexual/romantic love, and "agape" which is unconditional or unselfish love. We can have all three feelings for one person or we may have one of the three for the people we love. Is God expecting too much of us, by advising that we should love one another? What type of love do we have for strangers; people we do not know? What kind of love do we have for the Lord? God has an agape love for us. He proved his love for us when he created us, and when he died on the cross for our sins, so that we can be reunited with him, if it were to be our will. The Bible is clear and it tells us that God is love. If we have not love in our hearts for people then there is no way that we can know God. Examine yourselves to see if you are in Christ. You will know if you are allowing the Lord to dwell in you, based on how you treat others.

Mission/Purpose

"Before God formed us in our mothers' wombs God knew us. Before we came forth out of the wombs, God determined our destiny and designed plans for our lives." (Jeremiah 1:5)
"God has made known to us the mystery of his will for our lives, according to His good pleasure which He has purposed in Himself." (Ephesians 1:9)

We ask God to reveal His purpose for our lives when we—

- Read the Bible
- Meditate on the Word of God
- Pray

Do you have any clue as to what your mission/purpose is? If you do not know what your mission/purpose is I suggest that you start reading your Bible; that will give you wisdom and knowledge; it will open your eyes and allow you to see things clearly; you must meditate on God's word and you must pray. Ask God to reveal to you what your purpose is, ask for him to give you guidance. Everything will become clear to you, if you focus on the three simple steps mentioned above. You must seek God to determine your purpose in life.

God revealed to me that my purpose in this life is to spread his word, assist the homeless, the poor, and the disadvantaged people of this world. I have a passion for working with the homeless. God has filled me with love and compassion; he has given me a spirit to give. He has made me an advocate of the poor. My mission is to encourage and build hope within individuals who feel hopeless. I tell the hopeless that there is a God, who cares about them and their situation. I inform them that it is not the ability they possess or ever will obtain that will give them success, but it is that which the Lord can do for them. If God is for you, who can be against you (Romans 8:31)? People need to be educated; they need to know how they can gain God's favor in their lives. God's word says, "If you abide in me, and my word abide in you, ye shall ask what you will, and it shall be done unto you (John 15:7). This scripture ensures that if we live our lives according to the word of God, if our lives are not contrary to the word of God then he will show us favor; he will favorably answer our petitions.

If you have prayed and God has revealed to you your purpose, but it seems to be too big for you to handle, than rest assured that God has revealed to you what he wants you to do. If God is in the plan it is usually a very big plan. God is able to do big things. Don't be afraid of the task that God has called you to. You must trust in God and believe that he will make away for you to achieve whatever mission he has assigned to you. If you are afraid and overwhelmed by what God has called you to do, pray and ask for courage and strength. If you ask, God will give you what you need in order to see you through.

I knew that God had called me to work with the homeless back in 2005 when From Darkness to Light was established, but instead of doing what God called me to. I accepted a job within Corporate America and relocated to Kentucky to do my will. I put God's plans on hold for approximately two years, and it would have been longer if God had not called me off the job. God gave me something to do and I decided to do what I wanted to do. I wasn't ready to totally surrender my will when I heard him calling. So many of us are not ready to yield our will to God and God is merciful, patient, and longsuffering with us. He gives us free will and he continues to plead with us through the Holy Spirit; pleading for our hearts. If God had not called me off the job I might still be there wasting time. Now that God has my full attention I am depending on God to bless the ministry because what he has called me to do cannot be done without him.

I was afraid of my mission and I am still afraid to do some of the things God has called me to do. I am not perfect and I struggle with the enormous task of spreading God's word and being an advocate of the homeless. I want to help everyone that is suffering, but realize that I am not able to reach everyone and I can't do anything without Jesus Christ. I was inspired by God to write this book and I know that God will get this information into the hands of those that he wants to have it. I am very excited about the path that God has directed me to, but I find myself in an unfamiliar and awkward place in life right now. I never really had to exercise my faith in God. God had always blessed me with decent jobs in order to take care of my financial responsibilities and myself. As of 09/03/ 08 I have really been exercising my faith in the Lord. You see, I lost my job on 09/03/08 and I am depending on God to take care of me and bless my ministry.

Who am I? Why has God called me to speak for him? I recognize now that God will use anyone that will allow God to take control and use them. Although I didn't immediately yield my will, I felt God calling me and I knew that I needed to do what he was calling me to do. Once I accepted the calling I instantly knew that I had made the right choice; everything about what I am doing feels right. Now that I am on the road to fulfilling the purpose that I have been called to fulfill, I can see God's favor in my life. God is pleased with the things that I am doing and he blesses me with the fruit of the spirit.

God has a wonderful purpose for each of us and we will never be satisfied in life, until we determine his purpose for our lives and fulfill that purpose. Remember, if you do not know what God has called you to do, start reading his word (the Bible). Make sure to meditate; contemplate, study, and spend time with God on a regular basis. You need to build up your relationship with God; you need to get to know him. How can you trust someone you do not know? In order for you to trust God, you must first know him and feel comfortable in his presence. You need to know how to communicate with God, therefore you must pray and pray often. Keep God on your mind. Praise him in the good times and the bad. If you only seek God when you are in trouble or when you are having a problem, you must change this behavior. You need to seek God daily. God must be supreme in your life. There is a purpose for your life. God has a mission he wants you to fulfill.

You are not here by accident/mistake. Spend time with God; get to know him, ask him to reveal his will for your life, and he will do just that.

Rest on the Sabbath

"Remember the Sabbath day, to keep it holy. Six days shalt thou labour, and do all thy work: But the seventh day is the Sabbath of the LORD thy God: in it thou shalt not do any work, thou, nor thy son, nor thy daughter, thy manservant, nor thy maidservant, nor thy cattle, nor thy stranger that is within thy gates: For in six days the LORD made heaven and earth, the sea, and all that in them is, and rested the seventh day: wherefore the LORD blessed the Sabbath day, and hallowed it." (Exodus 20:8-11) The Sabbath is declared a day of rest and convocation.

God requested that we keep the Seventh Day Holy. At the beginning of time when he created the earth he sanctified the day and hollowed it; you can read about it in the first chapter of the book of Genesis. God knew that we would forget to keep the Seventh Day Holy, therefore God reminded use to keep the day Holy, by including the 4th commandment in his moral laws, which were written with God's finger. Many will say that Jesus did away with the law to keep the Seventh Day Sabbath when he came and died on the cross for our sins, but this could not be further from the truth. Jesus did not come to destroy the law, but to fulfill the law (Matthew 5:17-19). Jesus tells us that he is the same yesterday, today, and forever. The Lord tells us that he is the Lord and he change not (Heb. 13:8, Malachi 3:6). In the New Testament the Bible clearly says that the Sabbath was made for man and not man for the Sabbath (Mark 2:27). The Sabbath is a sign that we worship God; it is a sign between God and his people (Ezekiel 20:12). God has asked that we keep the day Holy and we ought to obey his command. Many people often confuse the moral law with the ceremonial law, which was written by Moses. The moral law was sacred; written on two tables of stone and put *into* the Ark of the Covenant. Again, God wrote the moral law with his very own finger and he has not done away with any portion of the moral law (The 10 commandments). The 4th commandment to keep the Sabbath Holy is a part of the moral law. When Jesus died on the cross for our sins the ceremonial law was done away with. The ceremonial law was written in a book by Moses, which was called "The Book of the Law." The hand of Moses wrote the book and it was placed on the *side* of the Ark. The book contained laws pertaining to ordinances, offerings, feast, new moons, ceremonial Sabbaths, etc. In the Bible (II Col 2:14, 16) the Apostle Paul said not to make the Gentiles keep the ceremonial law; he said to blot out ordinances, but he never said anything about doing away with God's moral law. The Apostles knew and understood that the moral law was to be kept. The following table will clarify between the Lord's Sabbath and the Ceremonial Sabbaths that were nailed to the cross.

The Lord's Sabbath	Ceremonial Sabbaths
Spoken by God personally (Exodus 20:1, 8-11)	Spoken by Moses (Exodus 24:3)
Written in stone by God Himself (Exodus 31:18)	Written by Moses hand on paper (Exodus 24:4)
Placed inside the Ark of the covenant (Deuteronomy 10:5)	Stored on the outside of the Ark (Deuteronomy 31:26)
Breaking the Sabbath is sin (1 John 3:4)	These were kept because of sin (See Leviticus)
It is a law of love (Matthew 22:35-40, Isaiah 58:13-14)	They were not love (Colossians 2:14, Galatians 4:9-10)
It is a law of liberty (freedom) (James 1:25, 2:10-12)	They were bondage (Galatians 4:9-10, Colossians 2:14)
Was established before sin (Genesis 2:1-3)	Were established after sin (Exodus 20:24)
Was made at creation (Genesis 2:1-3)	Were made after Sinai (Exodus 20:24)
The Sabbath is for everyone (Mark 2:27)	Only for the children of Israel & Jews (Read Old Testament)
God calls it MY Sabbath (Exodus 31:13, Ezekiel 20:20)	God calls it HER sabbaths (Hosea 2:11, Lamentations 1:7)
The Sabbath is eternal (Psalms 111:7-8, Isaiah 66:22-23)	Were nailed to the cross (Colossians 2:14, Ephesians 2:15)

Table 1. (See Appendix 1—Resources)

The current day that many worship on (Sunday) is an example of a significant number of Christians who are unaware that some of the beliefs in Christian Churches have originated from manmade traditions and paganism. Sunday worship originated from sun worship, which is why we have the pagan name SUN-day. Some claim that the Seventh Day Sabbath was changed to Sunday in order to honor the resurrection. History confirms that all Christians worshipped on Saturday until at least 120 AD, but many changed their day of worship in fear of persecution for Judaism. In the fourth century millions died during the Dark Ages for refusing to worship on Sunday which had been made the law. The fear of persecution caused all with the exception of approximately five hundred denominations to worship on Sunday. These facts regarding Sunday worship can be researched and proven in our history books. Many Christians have not bothered to research these facts, and they continue to follow manmade traditions and paganism.

The Sabbath Day was given to us at creation and it was made a moral law on the Mountain of Sinai. The Sabbath Day was kept by God's people and also kept by Jesus. The disciples honored the Sabbath Day and the day represents a sign of God's power. The Sabbath Day is a memorial to God; it honors his creation. God set the day apart from the other six days; he sanctified the day and he hollowed it. God has placed special blessing on the Sabbath Day and again he has asked that we keep it Holy. We must study to show ourselves approved, rightly dividing the word of truth (II Timothy 2:15). We must make sure to let no man deceive us when it comes to God's word (Matthew 24:4). Man will say and teach things that are contrary to God's word. The Bible tells us that we must study and understand the word for ourselves. God says that heaven and earth shall pass away, but his word shall not pass away (Matthew 24:35). We can count on God's word. God's word is sacred; therefore we must honor his word, no matter what men may say. God knew that man would seek to change times and laws (Daniel 7:25), which would confuse his people regarding which day is his Holy Sabbath Day. The Bible is clear about which day God has called us to keep holy, although man is teaching something contrary to God's word.

There are many Christians worshiping on Sunday, the 1st day of the week and they do not understand that they are disobeying God by doing so. If we were studying to show ourselves approved as God called us to do, there would be no questions about which day is God's Holy Sabbath. Many people are not familiar with the Sabbath, but when truth is presented to them it is up to them to accept the truth and do things according to God's will and not their own. Many would be convicted that they should worship on God's true Sabbath (Saturday), if they would only study the Lord's word and ask God to reveal what he would have them to do about the Sabbath. The Lord asked us to remember the Sabbath because he knew that we would forget and he knows that if we would keep the Sabbath the way he has commanded us to, it would draw us closer to him.

God has called us to keep the Sabbath and his word says, "If you keep your feet from breaking the Sabbath and from doing as you please on my holy day, if you call the Sabbath a delight and the Lord's holy day honorable, and if you honor it by not going your own way and not doing as you please or speaking idle words, then you will find your joy in the Lord, and it will cause you to ride on the heights of the land and to feast on the inheritance of your father Jacob. The mouth of the Lord has spoken (Isaiah 58: 13-14)."

I am a Sabbath keeper, but I have not allows kept the Sabbath, as I discussed in Chapter 1 (From Darkness to Light). It is very essential for Sabbath keepers to honor the Lord's Holy Sabbath Day. There are many who profess to be Sabbath keepers, but they do not keep the Sabbath in the way that the Lord has instructed. There are many who do not try to honor God's will, even though they may believe that God sanctified the Sabbath and asked that we honor it. Some Sabbath keepers are hypocrites and they conduct themselves in the way that is not acceptable to God. I would have been considered a hypocrite before my eyes were open, prior to my From Darkness to Light experience. I knew of the Sabbath and I believed that God sanctified it and asked us to keep it holy, but I was not allowing the Lord's holy word (the Bible) to convict me of the truth, therefore I was keeping my will and not God's will.

We must be careful not to grieve the Holy Spirit, if we find ourselves constantly performing our will instead of God's will, especially when we know right from wrong. The person who knows the truth and does not honor it may be in worse shape then the person who is not aware of the truth. We should all be thankful for God's mercy and his grace. Our God is a loving God, and he is long-suffering. God has given us such a blessing in the Sabbath, but many do not realize or recognize it. I ask that you study your Bible; do your research when it comes to the Sabbath. "Study to shew thyself approved unto God, a workman that needeth not to be ashamed, rightly dividing the word of truth (II Timothy 2:15)."

Eat Healthy

"Know ye not that ye are the temple of God, and that the Spirit of God dwelleth in you? If any man defile the temple of God, him shall God destroy; for the temple of God is holy, which temple ye are." (I Corinthians 3:16-17)

There is a familiar saying that "you are what you eat." There are positive and negative results associated with our eating habits. Food can be considered life sustaining and also life threatening, depending on how we as individuals consume it. Some foods are good for our health and some are considered bad. The Bible is clear and gives instruction and warning about specific foods to stay away from. God created us and he knows what is best for us, if we would simply adhere to Gods words we would be free from many of the illnesses (cancer, diabetes, hypertension, etc...) that are food related, which plague us today.

Again, God knows best when it comes to our health, after all he made us. The Bible tells us which foods are good for us to eat. You can find biblical guidance regarding food in the book of Leviticus and Deuteronomy. If we were to adhere to

God's instruction we would be healthier and better off. The Bible advises that we should not eat the blood or the fat of an animal. There are diseases in both the fat and the blood. (Leviticus 3:16-17, 7:23-24). The Bible offers a list of good and bad food and instructs us to stay away from the bad foods.

Some clean animals that are okay to eat; these animals part the hoof, are cloven footed, and chew the cud:
- Cow
- Deer
- Lamb
- Caribou
- Buffalo
- Elk
- Goat
- Moose

Fish that have fins and scales are clean:
- Bass
- Bluefish
- Crappie
- Perch
- Pike
- Salmon
- Sunfish
- Trout

Birds that are clean:
- Chicken
- Turkey
- Pheasant
- Grouse
- Quail

Clean creeping animals:
- Locusts
- Cricket
- Grasshopper

Some animals that are unclean and not safe to eat; these animals do not part the hoof, are not cloven footed, and do not chew the cud:
- Pig (pork)
- Rabbit
- Raccoon
- Squirrel
- Monkey
- Dog
- Coyote
- Fox
- Wolf
- Lion
- Tiger
- Horse
- Mule
- Zebra
- Bear

- Camel
- Elephant
- Llama
- Hippo
- Kangaroo

Water animals that do not have fins and scales:
- Catfish
- Eel
- Marlin
- Shark
- Abalone
- Clam
- Crab
- Crayfish
- Lobster
- Oyster
- Shrimp
- Jellyfish
- Squid
- Dolphin
- Seal
- Whale

Unclean Birds:
- Bat
- Eagle
- Osprey
- Raven
- Duck

- Swan
- Vulture

Unclean creeping animals:
- Frog
- Toad
- Crocodile
- Lizard
- Snake
- Turtle
- Salamander
- Newt
- Snail

We learn from reading the Bible that Daniel the prophet refused to eat King Nebuchadnezzar's meat and wine, instead he maintained a diet of pulse (vegetable food) and he was healthier; fairer and fatter than the King's men (Daniel 1: 1-16). It has been proven that following the Bible diet will keep us healthier and promote longevity. Eating whole grains, fresh fruits, and vegetables is the best diet for our human bodies. There are so many benefits from eating these foods. The closer we keep are diet to the earth (eating things grown from the earth; grains, fruits, and vegetables) the better off we will be. There has been many studies performed, boasting of the healing power of natural foods.

Regarding God's word pertaining to food, many would say that we no longer need to keep the food laws of the Bible. Man will say that the laws were done away with, but this is far from the truth. The Lord informed us of the food laws for a reason.

God knows what is best for us to eat. God made all things and he knows which foods would be harmful to our health and that is why he has given strict instruction on what we can and cannot eat. The Lord has not changed his mind regarding his instructions pertaining to what we can and cannot eat. The Bible says, "Jesus is the same yesterday, today and forever (Hebrews 13:8)." In Malachi 3:6 the Bible says, "I am the Lord, I change not." The Lord has not done away with the food laws. God knew that man would seek to change his law (Daniel 7:25), therefore he made provision; he left us with his word, in order to reveal his truth when it comes to how we should conduct ourselves. He has left instruction on what we can and cannot eat, how we should take care of our bodies (our temples), how we should pray, how we should live, etc. Everything we need to know is in the word of God. The Bible is full of wisdom and knowledge. If we choose not to read the word of God we are being foolish and the bible says, the foolish shall not stand in his sight. He says that he hates all workers of iniquity (Psalms 5:5). Ecclesiastes 7:17 says, "Be not over wicked, neither be thou foolish: why shouldest thou die before thy time?"

The Bible instructs us not to eat unclean foods, therefore we should not eat unclean meats, but we seem to have a habit of doing what we want in spite of what God says. It has been customary for us to discard the parts of the Bible we do not like or do not want to adhere to. For better understanding, please study Leviticus Chapter 11 (clean and unclean meats). Many say that God's law to eat healthy is an ordinance (decree, dogma, ceremonial law) that was nailed to the cross when Jesus died. The Ceremonial Laws with its sacrificial system pointed people to the coming of Christ and when Christ died on the cross the Ceremonial Law or the Mosaic Law was nailed to the cross; ending the sacrificial system. Colossians 2:14-16 says, "Blotting out the handwriting of ordinances that was against us, which was contrary to us, and took it out of the way, nailing it to his cross; And having spoiled principalities and powers, he made a shew of them openly, triumphing over them in it. Let no man therefore judge you in meat, or in drink, or in respect of an holyday, or of the new moon, or of the sabbath days." This passage is one of the most misunderstood within the entire Bible.

Many feel that Colossians 2:14-16 is saying that the Sabbath and the food laws regarding clean and unclean meats were done away with, but this is not true. If we would study our Bibles we would understand that the food laws are not apart of the Ceremonial Law and neither is the 4th Commandment, to keep the Sabbath Day Holy. Colossians 2:14-16 is not referring to the 4th Commandment Sabbath, but to the Ceremonial Sabbath Days and there were many; Passover, Feast of Weeks, etc. The passage is not referring to clean and unclean meats. The passage does not mention clean or unclean meats. The passage is referring to meat and drink offerings. If this passage were talking about clean and unclean meats it would be out of context, based on what is being discussed in Chapter 2. Again this passage is referring to meat and drink sacrifices and offerings (Hebrews 9:7-14 discuss such offerings).

Romans Chapter 14 talks about eating and drinking. It talks about one who may eat all things (meaning herbs and meats) and one who may eat herbs. In verse 5 the word says let every man be fully persuaded in his own mind. We must understand that the Lord is referring to clean meats and unfermented wine in this discussion held in Romans Chapter 14. The Lord has already instructed us not to eat unclean meats and not to drink strong drink or fermented wine in the Book of Leviticus. He has already advised which meats are okay to be eaten and what drink (unfermented wine) is okay for us to drink. Therefore, when Romans 14:2-3 says, "For one believeth that he may eat all things: another, who is weak, eateth herbs. Let not him that eateth despise him that eateth not; and let not him which eateth not judge him that eateth: for God hath received him." Again, we must understand that some people feel that we should not eat animals and we should only eat herbs, but God has given us the okay to eat clean meats, if we so choose to. Many feel Romans Chapter 14 gives them the right to eat anything they please, including unclean meats and this is just not so. The Bible says that we should study to show ourselves approved unto God, a workman that need not to be ashamed, rightly dividing the word of truth (II Timothy 2:15).

Be Content

"Let your conversation be without covetousness; and be content with such things as ye have for he hath said, I will never leave thee, nor forsake thee." (Hebrews 13:5)

Timothy advised the Hebrews not to dwell on things they did not have, but to be content with the things they did have. Timothy advised the Hebrews that their conversations should not be about greed, materialism, and gain. He advised the Hebrews that the Lord would never leave or forsake them. The words Timothy spoke to the Hebrews still apply to us today. If you are constantly focused on how you can "build an empire" or gain more, if you are not content in life, then you need to evaluate your walk with Christ.

I have struggled in this area. I know that greed and materialism can have negative effects and serious consequences on an individual's life. I have not always been content in life and I allowed my greed and desire for personal gain to set me on a path of struggle and constant explanation of character. Shortly after turning 18 years old, I was involved in a crime of petty theft, prior to this petty theft experience I had not always been forthcoming and had stolen things when I was a young child, between the ages of 7 and 9, which I explained in Chapter 1 (From Darkness to Light). At 18 years old I was convicted of a misdemeanor for stealing clothes from a department store. I was involved in a petty theft crime against a popular department store. A girlfriend accompanied me to the store and we were both charged with petty theft. I know for sure that we would not have committed the crime had we not been together; we encouraged each other to do it; we definitely talked each other into doing it. I remember having nightmares about us being prosecuted and having our records tarnished for life. I had vowed to stay on the straight and narrow after that. I was going off to college the fall of 1988 and was planning to study criminal justice. I wanted to become a Judge. I was planning to have my petty theft record expunged, but that never occurred. In my early twenties I committed a serious illegal offense, which caused my character and integrity to again be questioned. As a young person I experienced a serious financial hardship, due to living way over my means. At an early age I was facing bankruptcy. I had always been taught that good credit was very important, and to me it represented the difference between poverty and wealth. I did not want to file bankruptcy, and I was determined to figure out away to avoid it. My bright idea was to create counterfeit checks and have a friend (same friend that was involved with the petty theft), who worked for the bank cash the checks for me. I would use the money to pay off my debts. The plan was not successful. Instead of having my friend cash the checks we decided to submit the counterfeit checks to several area banks. We were able to cash all the checks that were submitted. The total amount received from the banks was approx. $2500. This money was to be used to pay my bills, but instead the money was used as restitution, after the offense was discovered and prosecuted by the police. I was actually afraid to spend the money and did not pay my bills right away. Even during this time of sin I know that the Lord was still watching over me and showing me favor. My conscience would not allow me to spend the money. Something inside was telling me not to spend any of it. I praise God for not allowing me to spend the money because when it was time to make restitution I was able to do so. I believe I would have been sentenced to serve jail time if I had not been able to make restitution. Again, I know that I would not have been able to make restitution, if I had used the money to pay my bills.

The bottom line is that I was not content. Greed and materialism had a lot to do with my behavior, and the things that I was involved in back then. I have completely changed my life for the better, but the things I did early on in life had serious consequences, and the choices I made back then still effect me today. I have missed out on many great career opportunities, do to the convictions/criminal record that I currently have. I have had some set backs, but finding the Lord in 2005 has been the best thing that has happened to me.

We all have a purpose in life. I am the perfect example that the Lord can still use a person, even though they may not be perfect and may have made some major mistakes in life. The Lord has blessed me abundantly! I have turned my life around, due to God's grace and mercy. I am now an advocate of working with the poor and giving back to the community. The Lord blessed me with a very rewarding career in the field of finance, even though there is a conviction of theft and counterfeiting on my record; I am a convicted felon. I could not have made any accomplishments without the Lord seeing me through. Only the Lord could make anything a possibility for me, considering I have a criminal record. The Lord has opened doors for me and I have had some very good jobs in the field of finance. I have been blessed with middle management positions and I have excelled regardless of my background. It has not been easy, but the Lord made away out of no way for me. Many would say that it would be impossible for somebody with my criminal background to obtain a middle management position in a credit and collection department with a wide range of responsibilities. I was responsible for overseeing the firm's issuance of credit, establishing credit-rating criteria, determining credit ceilings, managing credit card fraud, managing third party collections, managing bankruptcy, and monitoring the collections of past due accounts. Again, many would say it would be impossible for me to secure jobs with this type of responsibility; especially considering my offense was related to theft and counterfeiting. God opened doors for me that no man could shut. I did not conceal any information in order to get any position. I have always been forthcoming and the Lord blessed my efforts.

My convictions occurred prior to me starting my career in accounting and finance; I was young when I obtained the convictions. In the early 1990's a member from my church allowed me to work with her doing some collection/accounts receivable work and thus this is how I got my start in finance. I enjoyed working in accounts receivables and later went on to obtain other great opportunities/positions within the field of finance, again God opened the doors.

I was young and naive and did not realize the struggle that I would endure, due to being a convicted felon. I made some serious mistakes early on and did not realize that those mistakes would hunt me for the rest of my life. In spite of my mistakes I have been determined not to let them hold me down. I found strength in God to continue fighting regardless of how many job rejections I received, and there has been hundreds. I have been blessed to work for companies that have not allowed really old convictions to hinder an applicant's chance of being considered for a position. Some of the applications I completed only wanted to know about felonies that were less than seven or ten years old. My convictions happened more than 2 decades ago. My highest paying position hired me, even though I informed that I had a felony. I explained what happened and at the time the felony was more than 15 years old. The company took a chance and hired me anyway. I was a model employee, giving 125%. I did an excellent job for the company.

God has given me a drive and spirit of achievement; I will not quit. The Lord allowed me to obtain my MBA and I am currently working on my Doctorate degree in organizational management. God has big plans for me and I will continue to seek his face. I am not sure what my next assignment will be, but I know that he has something awesome waiting for me. It is through prayer and studying that I am able to endure. My personal relationship with God makes everything okay. When I think of my background and the positions I have held, I think of Abraham's question, "Is anything too hard for the Lord (Genesis 18:14)?

God has blessed me and I will not complain. I recently lost my last job (Sept. 2008) and I have been seeking God's face because I know that he has something special that he wants me to do. I truly feel that God called me off the job in order to focus on my ministry (From Darkness to Light). I am currently unemployed and actively seeking employment because I am required to do so. I have been having a really hard time finding a position because God has decided to keep the doors closed. When my position was eliminated I was not worried about finding another job because I knew that there was a reason God called me off the job. I feel that God has something much better for me. I am now seeking God and waiting on him to reveal his plans for the next chapter of my life.

We cannot allow life's circumstances to keep us down. We must praise God no matter our circumstances and he will bless us. We cannot allow people, jobs, or things to define who we are. Our worth is not within people, jobs, or any material thing. A job title, the house you live in, the car you drive, the man or woman you date, or the amount of money you have in your bank account does not make you better or less than the next person. God decides our worth and we are worth more than gold in his eyes no matter our status. God is not a respecter of person (Acts 10:34).

I have always loved the Lord even during the time that I was doing wrong. I knew that I was doing wrong when I committed the offenses. God made a way of escape and I did not choose to take it. I felt horrible then, and I feel horrible now that I did not do what was right. I let God down back then. I did not have a strong relationship with the Lord back then, but I am thankful for God's mercy and grace. God gives us all free will and we do not always make the right choices in life. I am thankful that God has used my experiences, my mistakes, my faults, etc to shape and mold my character. I am pleased with the outcome. Although I made some serious and stupid mistakes the Lord has worked all things together for my good. Romans 8:28 says, "And we know that in all things God works for the good of those who love him, who have been called according to his purpose." God has called me to speak on his behalf even though I have baggage and have not lived a perfect Christian life. I must stress the fact that God can use anyone to further his cause. I have dedicated the rest of my life to spreading the gospel, being a servant, working with the poor, the disenfranchised, and the disadvantaged.

Again, God is not a respecter of person (Acts 10:34). He does not care if you are black or white, rich or poor. He wants you to worship and praise him. He is willing to work with anyone that is willing to work with him, but you have to be sincere. There is hope for all, if the Lord can forgive me for the things I did and allow me to speak for him he can do the same for you; it does not matter what you have done in the past. If you would review the lives of the disciples and apostles you will see that they were far from perfect. I have learned to be content with the things that I have. I have learned to live within my means. The Lord has given me the fruit of the spirit, which allows me to be at peace and content with his blessings. I no longer take things for granted. I am truly blessed and I recognize the blessings and realize where they are coming from. I can say that there is nothing to hard for God.

Fruit of the Spirit

"But the fruit of the Spirit is love, joy, peace, longsuffering, gentleness, goodness, faith, meekness, temperance: against such there is no law." (Galatians 5:22-23) The Lord promises to give us the fruits of the spirit. *"Thou wilt keep him in perfect peace, whose mind is stayed on thee: because he trusteth in thee." (Isaiah 26:3).*

Jesus says, "I am the true vine, and my Father is the vinedresser. Every branch of mine that bears no fruit, he takes away, and every branch that does bear fruit he prunes, that it may bear more fruit. You are already made clean by the word which I have spoken to you. Abide in me, and I in you. **As the branch cannot bear fruit by itself, unless it abides in the vine, neither can you, unless you abide in me.** *I am the vine, you are the branches. He who abides in me, and I in him, he it is that bears much fruit, for apart from me you can do nothing. If a man does not abide in me, he is cast forth as a branch and withers; and the branches are gathered, thrown into the fire and burned. If you abide in me, and my words abide in you, ask whatever you will, and it* *shall be done for you. By this my Father is glorified, that you bear much fruit, and so prove to be my disciples."* (John 15:1-8, NIT)

Understand that you will become a very wealthy individual, if God bestow upon you the fruit of the spirit. Only God can extend the spirit of love, joy, peace, longsuffering, gentleness, goodness, faith, meekness, and temperance. All the money in the world cannot buy these attributes or characteristics. Money maybe able to buy temporary joy and happiness, but it cannot buy anything permanent, only God can give the fruit of the spirit. If you wish to acquire the fruit of the spirit all you need to do is ask. God will give you his Holy Spirit and he will also give you the fruit of the spirit, which is the answer/cure for any problem or concern you may have. God is the answer to any concern, no matter how big or small. If you are heart broken, he can mend your broken heart and provide love, if you are depressed he can give you joy, if you are worried or concerned about life struggles he can give you peace. Again, only God can give you lasting love, joy, peace, longsuffering, gentleness, goodness, faith, meekness, and temperance. Money can not buy lasting love, joy, peace, etc.

When Christians are walking in the Holy Spirit, they will produce the fruit of the spirit. They will start to show characteristics and attributes of having the fruit of life. They will be transformed and will become more like Jesus. The nine fruit mentioned are all characteristics of God. Christians should study the fruit and develop it. The Bible says, "Ask and it shall be given you; seek, and ye shall find; knock, and it shall be opened unto you." (Matthew 7:7).

An article (All About God) found on-line describes the nine biblical attributes; the 9 fruit of the spirit: **Love**—"And so we know and rely on the love God has for us. God is love. Whoever lives in love lives in God, and God in him" (1 John 4:16). Through Jesus Christ, our greatest goal is to do all things in love. "Love is patient, love is kind. It does not envy, it does not boast, it is not proud. It is not rude, it is not self-seeking, it is not easily angered, it keeps no record of wrongs. Love does not delight in evil but rejoices with the truth. It always protects, always trusts, always hopes, always perseveres. Love never fails" (1 Corinthians 13:4-8). **Joy**—"The joy of the Lord is your strength" (Nehemiah 8:10). "Let us fix our eyes on Jesus, the author and perfecter of our faith, who for the joy set before him endured the cross, scorning its shame, and sat down at the right hand of the throne of God" (Hebrews 12:2). **Peace**—"Therefore, since we have been justified through faith, we have peace with God through our Lord Jesus Christ" (Romans 5:1). "May the God of hope fill you with all joy and peace as you trust in him, so that you may overflow with hope by the power of the Holy Spirit" (Romans 15:13). **Longsuffering** (patience)—We are "strengthened with all might, according to his glorious power, unto all patience and longsuffering with joyfulness" (Colossians 1:11). "With all lowliness and meekness, with longsuffering, forbearing one another in love" (Ephesians 4:2). **Gentleness** (kindness)—We should live "in purity, understanding, patience and kindness; in the Holy Spirit and in sincere love; in truthful speech and in the power of God; with weapons of righteousness in the right hand and in the left" (2 Corinthians 6:6-7). **Goodness**—"Wherefore also we pray always for you, that our God would count you worthy of this calling, and fulfill all the good pleasure of his goodness, and the work of faith with power" (2 Thessalonians 1:11). "For the fruit of the Spirit is in all goodness and righteousness and truth" (Ephesians 5:9). **Faith** (faithfulness)— "O Lord, thou art my God; I will exalt thee, I will praise thy name; for thou hast done wonderful things; thy counsels of old are faithfulness and truth" (Isaiah 25:1). "I pray that out of his glorious riches he may strengthen you with power through his Spirit in your inner being, so that Christ may dwell in your hearts through faith" (Ephesians 3:16-17). **Meekness**— "Brethren, if a man be overtaken in a fault, ye which are spiritual, restore such an one in the spirit of meekness; considering thyself, lest thou also be tempted" (Galatians 6:1). "With all lowliness and meekness, with longsuffering, forbearing one another in love" (Ephesians 4:2). **Temperance** (self-control)—"But also for this very reason, giving all diligence, add to your faith virtue, to virtue knowledge, to knowledge self-control, to self-control perseverance, to perseverance godliness, to godliness brotherly kindness, and to brotherly kindness love" (2 Peter 1:5-7) (http:// www.allaboutgod.com/fruit-of-the-spirit.htm).

The outcome of a "from darkness to light" experience is the fruit of the spirit. A from darkness to light experience is actually becoming born again. When a person (Christian) becomes born again they become a new person and you will see things change in their life. They will take off the old man and put on the new man (Ephesians 4:22-24). When a person starts to seek the things of God and ask him to come into their life they will wake up and begin to know the Lord for themselves. They will gain wisdom and knowledge. Their eyes will be opened and they will start to let their light shine, and others will be able to see a difference. The Christian will recognize what needs to be done to strengthen their walk with Jesus Christ. The Christian will recognize that they need Jesus and their faith will be developed and strengthened. The Christian will become more and more like Jesus and his/her love will grow. God is love and we are shaped in his image, therefore when we allow ourselves to be on one accord with our Heavenly Father our characters will emulate the first fruit of the spirit, which is Love. The Christian will have a desire to please the Lord and they will determine what their purpose in life is. The Christian will seek to please God and will keep his commandments, doing everything that is pleasing to God; worshiping him, keeping the Sabbath, eating well in order to stay healthy. If we have truly been born again, whatever God has asked us to do, is not too much for us to do; we would try to honor his will, using his strength to do so.

The Lord will bless those who are seeking him with their whole heart; he will give them the Holy Spirit and the Holy Spirit will provide the fruit of his spirit, which will allow for contentment. If we can be content here on earth we will be considered very prosperous in the eyes of many. Having the Holy Spirit is truly a blessing and it is God's promise to us, but we must claim the blessing (Luke 11:9-13). Make sure not to be anxious for the things of this world. Make sure to seek the kingdom of God first and all things needed will be provided to you (Luke 12:22-31). God wants to enhance our personalities with 9 fruit of the Holy Spirit; God wishes to transmit or pass on this fruit in order to mold/shape our Character after him. It is my prayer that God would allow you to experience a "from darkness to light" experience. I pray that we will all be ready to meet Jesus Christ in the clouds of glory (1 Thessalonians 4:15-18). Amen.

Appendix 1
Resources

Johnson, Sharon. Wolves in the American Church 2007

Ellen G. White. Steps to Christ

Table 1. http://www.ceremoniallaw.com/

All About God. Fruit of the Spirit—The Nine Biblical Attributes.   http://www.allaboutgod.com/fruit-of-the-spirit.htm

The Holy Bible (KJV) and http://www.biblegateway.com/

Appendix 2
Bible Translations

*(All translations are from the King James Version,
unless otherwise noted.)*

(Deuteronomy 4:29 NAS).
But from there you will seek the LORD your God, and you will find Him if you search for Him with all your heart and all your soul.

(Isaiah 55:8-9)
"For my thoughts are not your thoughts, neither are your ways my ways," declares the LORD. "As the heavens are higher than the earth, *so are my ways higher than your ways and my thoughts than your thoughts"*

(Proverbs 3: 5-6)
"Trust in the LORD with all thine heart; and lean not unto thine own understanding. In all thy ways acknowledge him, and he shall direct thy paths."

(John 14:6)
Jesus saith unto him, I am the way, the truth, and the life: no man cometh unto the Father, but by me.

(Revelation 2:7)
He that hath an ear, let him hear what the Spirit saith unto the churches; To him that overcometh will I give to eat of the tree of life, which is in the midst of the paradise of God.

Luke 6:32
For if ye love them which love you, what thank have ye? For sinners also love those that love them.

Luke 9:26
If anyone is ashamed of me and my words, the Son of Man will be ashamed of him when he comes in his glory and in the glory of the Father and of the holy angels.

Mat 10:33
But whoever disowns me before men, I will disown him before my Father in heaven.

Acts 10:34
Then Peter opened his mouth, and said, of a truth I perceive that God is no respecter of persons.

Mat 7:7
Ask, and it shall be given you; seek, and ye shall find; knock, and it shall be opened unto you.

Mat 7:16
Ye shall know them by their fruits. Do men gather grapes of thorns, or figs of thistles?

Mat 7:20
Wherefore by their fruits ye shall know them.

Luke 11:9
And I say unto you, Ask, and it shall be given you; seek, and ye shall find; knock, and it shall be opened unto you.

John 12:32
And I, if I be lifted up from the earth, will draw all men unto me.

II Corinthians 5:17
Therefore if any man be in Christ, he is a new creature: old things are passed away; behold, all things are become new.

(John 15:7)
If ye abide in me, and my word abide in you, ye shall ask what ye will and it shall be done unto you."

(Heb. 10:23)
"Pray, believe, rejoice, sing praises to God because he has answered your prayers. Take him at his word. He is faithful that promised."

Isaiah 26:3
Thou wilt keep him in perfect peace, whose mind is stayed on thee: because he trusteth in thee.

Romans 8:28
And we know that in all things God works for the good of those who love him, who have been called according to his purpose.

Romans 8:31
What shall we then say to these things? If God be for us, who can be against us?

Timothy 6:10
For the love of money is the root of all-evil.

II Timothy 2:15
Study to shew thyself approved unto God, a workman that needeth not to be ashamed, rightly dividing the word of truth.

I Thessalonians 5:17
Pray without ceasing

Matthew 7: 21-23
21Not every one that saith unto me, Lord, Lord, shall enter into the kingdom of heaven; but he that doeth the will of my Father, which is in heaven.

22Many will say to me in that day, Lord, Lord, have we not prophesied in thy name? and in thy name have cast out devils? and in thy name done many wonderful works?

23And then will I profess unto them, I never knew you: depart from me, ye that work iniquity.

I Corinthians 11:1 (NIV)
Follow my example, as I follow the example of Christ.

II Timothy 1: 8-10 (NKJV)
8 Therefore do not be ashamed of the testimony of our Lord, nor of me His prisoner, but share with me in the sufferings for the gospel according to the power of God, 9 who has saved us and called *us* with a holy calling, not according to our works, but according to His own purpose and grace which was given to us in Christ Jesus before time began, 10 but has now been revealed by the appearing of our Savior Jesus Christ, *who* has abolished death and brought life and immortality to light through the gospel,

(Acts 3:19)
Repent ye therefore, and be converted, that your sins may be blotted out, when the times of refreshing shall come from the presence of the Lord.

(Romans 12:19)
For it is written, vengeance is mine; I will repay, saith the Lord.

Proverbs 20:22
Do not say I'll pay you back for this wrong! Wait for the Lord, and He will deliver you.

(Ephesians 1:3-5)
(3) Blessed *be* the God and Father of our Lord Jesus Christ, who has blessed us with every spiritual blessing in the heavenly *places* in Christ, (4) just as He chose us in Him before the foundation of the world, that we should be holy and without blame before Him in love, (5) having predestined us to adoption as sons by Jesus Christ to Himself, according to the good pleasure of His will.

(Hebrews 13:20-21)
(20) Now the God of peace, that brought again from the dead our Lord Jesus, that great shepherd of the sheep, through the blood of the everlasting covenant, (21) Make you perfect in every good work to do his will, working in you that which is well pleasing in his sight, through Jesus Christ; to whom be glory for ever and ever. Amen.

(Hebrews 11:6)
But without faith it is impossible to please him: for he that cometh to God must believe that he is, and that he is a rewarder of them that diligently seek him.

(Colossians 2:6)
As you therefore have received Christ Jesus the Lord, so walk ye in him.

(Jeremiah 31:3)
I have loved thee with an everlasting love: therefore with loving-kindness have I drawn thee

(Isaiah 58: 13-14)

13) If you keep your feet from breaking the Sabbath and from doing as you please on my holy day, if you call the Sabbath a delight and the Lord's holy day honorable, and if you honor it by not going your own way and not doing as you please or speaking idle words,

14) Then you will find your joy in the Lord, and it will cause you to ride on the heights of the land and to feast on the inheritance of your father Jacob. The mouth of the Lord has spoken.

(John 14:15)

"If you love me," Jesus said, "you will obey what I command."

(1 John 2:3-4)

If we know Christ, we obey his commands.

(John 13:34)

A new commandment I give unto you, That ye love one another; as I have loved you, that ye also love one another.

(Matthew 22:36-38)

Master, which is the great commandment in the law? Jesus said unto him, Thou shalt love the Lord thy God with all thy heart, and with all thy soul, and with all thy mind. This is the first and great commandment.

(Exodus 20:8-11)

Remember the sabbath day, to keep it holy. Six days shalt thou labour, and do all thy work: But the seventh day is the Sabbath of the LORD thy God: in it thou shalt not do any work, thou, nor thy son, nor thy daughter, thy manservant, nor thy maidservant, nor thy cattle, nor thy stranger that is within thy gates: For in six days the LORD made heaven and earth, the sea, and all that in them is, and rested the seventh day: wherefore the LORD blessed the Sabbath day, and hallowed it.

The Sabbath is declared a day of rest and convocation.

(I Corinthians 3:16-17)
Know ye not that ye are the temple of God, and that the Spirit of God dwelleth in you? If any man defile the temple of God, him shall God destroy; for the temple of God is holy, which temple ye are.

(Galatians 5:22-23)
"But the fruit of the Spirit is love, joy, peace, longsuffering, gentleness, goodness, faith, meekness, temperance: against such there is no law."

(John 15:1-8, NIT)
"I am the true vine, and my Father is the vinedresser. Every branch of mine that bears no fruit, he takes away, and every branch that does bear fruit he prunes, that it may bear more fruit. You are already made clean by the word which I have spoken to you. Abide in me, and I in you. As the branch cannot bear fruit by itself, unless it abides in the vine, neither can you, unless you abide in me. I am the vine, you are the branches. He who abides in me, and I in him, he it is that bears much fruit, for apart from me you can do nothing. If a man does not abide

in me, he is cast forth as a branch and withers; and the branches are gathered, thrown into the fire and burned. If you abide in me, and my words abide in you, ask whatever you will, and it shall be done for you. By this my Father is glorified, that you bear much fruit, and so prove to be my disciples."

(Jeremiah 1:5)
"Before God formed us in our mothers' wombs God knew us. Before we came forth out of the wombs, God determined our destiny and designed plans for our lives."

(Ephesians 1:9)
"God has made known to us the mystery of his will for our lives, according to His good pleasure which He has purposed in Himself."

Leviticus 3:16-17
(16) And the priest shall burn them upon the altar: it is the food of the offering made by fire for a sweet savour: all the fat is the LORD's. (17) It shall be a perpetual statute for your generations throughout all your dwellings, that ye eat neither fat nor blood.

Leviticus 7:23-24
(23) Speak unto the children of Israel, saying, Ye shall eat no manner of fat, of ox, or of sheep, or of goat. (24) And the fat of the beast that dieth of itself, and the fat of that which is torn with beasts, may be used in any other use: but ye shall in no wise eat of it.

Hebrews 13:8
Jesus is the same yesterday, today and forever.

Malachi 3:6
I am the Lord, I change not.

II Cor. 13:5
Examine yourselves, whether ye be in the faith; prove your own selves. Know ye not your own selves, how that Jesus Christ is in you, except ye be reprobates?

(Psalm 100:3).
"Know you that the LORD he is God: it is he that has made us, and not we ourselves; we are his people, and the sheep of his pasture"

(I Cor. 10:13)
There hath no temptation taken you but such as is common to man: but God is faithful, who will not suffer you to be tempted above that ye are able; but will with the temptation also make a way to escape, that ye may be able to bear it.

I John 1:9
If we confess our sins he is faithful and just to forgive us of our sins, and to cleanse us from all unrighteousness

Luke 11:9-13
(9) I say unto you, Ask, and it shall be given you; seek, and ye shall find; knock, and it shall be opened unto you.

(10) For every one that asketh receiveth; and he that seeketh findeth; and to him that knocketh it shall be opened.

(11) If a son shall ask bread of any of you that is a father, will he give him a stone? or if he ask a fish, will he for a fish give him a serpent?

(12) Or if he shall ask an egg, will he offer him a scorpion?

(13) If ye then, being evil, know how to give good gifts unto your children: how much more shall your heavenly Father give the Holy Spirit to them that ask him?

Luke 12:22-31

(22) And he said to his disciples, "Therefore I tell you, do not be anxious about your life, what you will eat, nor about your body, what you will put on.

(23) For life is more than food, and the body more than clothing.

(24) Consider the ravens: they neither sow nor reap, they have neither storehouse nor barn, and yet God feeds them. Of how much more value are you than the birds!

(25) And which of you by being anxious can add a single hour to his span of life?

(26) If then you are not able to do as small a thing as that, why are you anxious about the rest?

(27) the lilies, how they grow: they neither toil nor spin, yet I tell you, even Solomon in all his glory was not arrayed like one of these.

(28) But if God so clothes the grass, which is alive in the field today, and tomorrow is thrown into the oven, how much more will he clothe you, O you of little faith!

(29) And do not seek what you are to eat and what you are to drink, nor be worried.

(30) For all the nations of the world seek after these things, and your Father knows that you need them.

(31) Instead, seek his kingdom, and these things will be added to you.

1 Thessalonians 4:15-18 (NIV)

(15) According to the Lord's own word, we tell you that we who are still alive, who are left till the coming of the Lord, will certainly not precede those who have fallen asleep.

(16) For the Lord himself will come down from heaven, with a loud command, with the voice of the archangel and with the trumpet call of God, and the dead in Christ will rise first.

(17) After that, we who are still alive and are left will be caught up together with them in the clouds to meet the Lord in the air. And so we will be with the Lord forever. (18) Therefore encourage each other with these words.

Misc. thoughts:

Obedience motivated by love

There is no limit to the love God has for us, who gave us his own Son in whom we have died to sin and now live in righteousness.